i speak to the poet in man

i speak to the poet in man

Q. R. Hand, Jr.

Jukebox Press
Oakland, California

No part of this book, may be reproduced in any form by any means, electronic or mechanical, including photo-copying, recording, or information retrieval system, without written permission from the publisher.

Grateful acknowledgement is hereby made to the following periodicals in which some of these poems have appeared:

Maybe Mombasa, New Bay View, North Mission News, Black Scholar, Clay Drum and Appeal to Reason.

Special thanks to Ralph LaCharity, Jim Queen, Victor Miller, Conyus, Bill Polak and John Bryant.

Library of Congress Catalogue Number: 84-081431
ISBN: 0932693-00-8

Copyright © 1985 by Quentin R. Hand, Jr.
All rights reserved.

*This book is dedicated to
Annie Laurie Chestnut
from all of us
with loving memories
of her.*

contents

i never used to end a poem   1
when i was in school   2
who signify what   6
hanging over   8
what remedy   10
getting better   11
looming   12
just 'cause   13
i speak to the poet in man   14
women and children first   22
scrambled   26
things are falling a part   28
jones town   29
whose city THERE   30
DEVOLUTION   34
how sweet it is   39
s & m lover   42
we used to sit like this   43
CAPRICORN   45
être rejeté   51

i never used to end a poem with a preposition

some times
i fill a room
with not me

like
i fill a poem
with not me

filling a role
prosaically

with some one else's
poetics

filled with nots
and which nots
and what nots
and how not to's

not me fill poem
i   some times
fill a room with

when i was in school

when i was in school
they made me a monitor
said i could look through
the hole in the desk and
view the rhapsodic theater
that seniors got to act in

i saw them kill the spanish rose daily
in the last hour of the gun

my teacher said i could be
punk of the month   next year
but when i told him i was
already exposed to terminal greed
they expelled me to the black hills
with a note that explained
mr magoo spent me
for a piece of the map

the hills needed no explanations
i was dumbfounded to learn

when i was in school
they gave me a cage
to carry basic questions around in
yelping and yammering about
the walk on parts of god and man

and i read within parentheses
littered with a glint of   a hint
of   a trace   of a place
stage directions
to the invisible man's shower
and what corners to cut
to get to an obie   young

(ducky wucky on the wall
  who's the farthest from a fall)

when i was in school
they declared a war
in so many languages i didn't understand
i couldn't fight in it

i would've loved to be a general
with double barrel machine guns in
my holsters and medals of honor
that glows in the dark

communiques   to fill a novel with
from the highest command there is

all those armies   at my beck and call

if they could've   just
had the kind of war
i could've been a soldier in

when i was in school they put a clock to lie on my wrist

gave me the what time is it itch

am i late   or now   or never
where do i find forever

is the moment righteous or just   right
according to that second hand which sneaks up
perversely behind your first stitch in time
and unravels doubt with perspicacity

leaves you holding in your hand
some profound truth to pound away

a way in to the night at a line
about a burst of busted meaning   and
where to   and whammy   and what color
was your mammy

and was her draw string   so tight
you could choke on all of her thighs   at one time
before the alarm could run down the milky way
and call you out at second base

who signify what

i am saying some thing
i am saying some thing
what is the some thing
i am saying saying
what is the some thing
the some thing
the some thing
some thing
some thing
some thing
some thing else
some thing else
some thing else is being said
some thing else is being heard
some thing else is being experienced
some thing is saying what
some thing is saying what
some thing is sayng what
saying what who
saying what who
what who
what who
what who is here
what who is here
what who is
what who is
what you is and what you ain't
both at the same time
what you is and what you ain't
is what you is all the time
some thing else
some thing else

some thing else is being said
some thing else is being said
on the cutting edge of who we are
when a some thing is being said
and we are of the saying
i am saying some thing
i am saying some thing
let's have another drink
let's have another conversation about
all the shit we keep taking
and what we're gonna do about it
when we get the right chance
what is the some thing
i am saying saying
what is the some thing
i am saying saying
and what is some thing else

hanging over

i felt like a lonesome end needing a periscope to find the huddle
i barked orders like the captain
all the while sipping from my back pocket
from my own so i thought private stock
fluid spiked with archaic sterilities

there had been fifths and quarts
gallons of this i of lanky martinet
ranging over the counters with an eye steady
on thematics of the transactions
machinations of currencies passed out by clerks
the real thing to certain receivers

i was sweet jesus going going gone
to beat the machine that eats the data
beat the machine that eats the dada
teeming feeding vectors of terror who
come at night and force a hand full of frights through each crack
in my plan

i was trying to spray them
running all over the floor
enforced obsolescences and me suspended
above in this colloid
collusions left and right
these our authorities
and my last thought
as i found my selves slipping in the toilet bowl
was order a gallon more

i threw up smoke screens
baked a cosmos in my bad breath
told my comforters talk to the seas about
street corner hungers and inter tribal friend ships
look your selves through lenses of ceremony and ritual
pastels of moments with flux and the brave
you see i am too busy to eat at the rite spot

i was vomiting skeletons of clean fictions
articulating bare gesture stern and bleak
leaving room only for listening to billie through bile
rank morphine sounds over and over i
sure need your heart to pull me out this time

what remedy

throw me a husk of zap
my belly's full of stainless steel
pirouettes and a purple pirahna
i hooked at the klee exhibit
'cause the guard issued me some license
when he saw me looking at you

i missed with my line and
stomached what i caught with glee
and lack of accuracy

getting better

it doesn't have to
come with pain
it just seems that way

you've got to learn to
stop pouncing and
try with all your heart
to not try

let the centipede
come to you
the way it will

do not watch it
inch and inch up
your leg and thigh

as it's about to
bite
grab quickly
open your hand
see lilies
their fields

loomin

her art and craft woven
into her design i am
spelled out in the stitches
of

a side of her
she needles with play
from time to time
lazily   smiling

just 'cause

i call her
two times   a day
she thinks she has me
running after her

what she doesn't know
is the thousand times
i don't

you think i want her
images sprinting to pay
the phone bill

i speak to the poet in man

listening to the calling of the cells
cornered in extremeties
named marauder

a prophet with no tongues
and dis embodied voice

nerve to sing the blues and latest news
together

glyphic cartoon clouds
bubble guts pow and whammo
time and dime store tunes

that break a guilty conscience down
to sock and garter
trepidations

i speak to the poet in man

words that paint sound
in viscosities
of that certain place
at that certain time

a calculus of memory in tones
where harmony is one space only
on a spectrum of ball and light

another variance in aweave

that velocitizes selectively
the figures of speech
and time
and place
and others smacking of being

and being is believing

i speak to the poet in man

check lists of terminologies
clinging to my finger tips
like putty

for cracks of minute catastrophe

a wrong declension

a detention of meanings
officially unapproved
come to register visible protest
in risible any ways

and
i rise to meet them
with
     i all ways tie my lines like this
     'cause a line is supposed to

     RIGHT!

i ask you
who laughs last

i speak to the poet in man

fugitive from splendid fates
sheen and mannered vehicles

whose slip and slide effects
glisten with soft and sledge hammer

packaged states of ecstasy
in cross town hiring halls
where masters bridge the difference
between your image and your flesh
with cold cash deductables

i speak to the poet in man

from minarets
shining blinding onyx
in a total eclipse of spirit

registering from heart to heart

leaning on the gate
lounging on the stoop

drinking the wine
of the time that dooms
sweet

and the wet
trickling down

i speak to the poet in man

even now

unfolding songs
in nights of blank

the shriek the moan ·
in teams of a lone

shuffling gauntlet
of moment and trick

meld of feign and less than self
whose hearing aids register stones
only

i speak to the poet in man

that barnacled yes

latching on
screwed in to each platelet
with sear and stench

gimme an inch more gotchas

generation after generation
leaving you scabbed with valentines

expensive offsprungoutofdirt
all dartedinandoutofgoodstuff

giving you hang overs for years
clutching like orange marmalade

the give that gave
neither in or out

aaaaaahhh   most amazing
stillgivingbirthto

creatures of the heart
with two backs and
the rack of separations

we are the people
of the sun

we are the people of the sun

glory morning peoples
of so many selves

sun gods
acry for the world

i speak to the poet in man

women and children first

the woogies are coming
constantly
all the time

the woogies are coming
defying laws of gravity
grave levities' flux
lexicons prancing
on the other side of the tracks

woogies
levitating on a pin
whose many heads speak
a multilingua franca
free a' bullshit
and the correlations' pellets

the woogies are coming
down the streets
in the fleet's pantry
behind the vaults
under the cells
everywhere
you look and see
through the cracks
defining faults
tip over the rock
at the top of the tree
spinning locks of grace
talking with visitors from out of sight
about the comings and goings
of raunchy spirits
who shoot craps on Saturn's rings
and snort asteroids for kicks
between the beat and its inception

there are woogies

in this night of threats
in overweening image
which structures productions
that pass for progress
as eskimos catapult barriers
to buy ice boxes
with hard earned trash
and the missionaries' zeal
and jungles grow cities
of glass
blinding indians in flight
selling their birthright
to a tribe of accountants
who pay in priceless mystifications
and the smile that lies

the woogies know by intuition
the demanding interstice
of the window and its sill
can walk a tight rope on d.t.'s
spill a can of diamonds
and not miss a drop
and talk to butterflies
in and out of the neighborhood

woogies dress in less than that
infiltrate panty hose
from either side
play backgammon with giraffes
with or without reservations
and infest every carnaval
on every plantation
with the primeval itch
that woogies cultivate
on another plane

woogie craft
woogie art
woogie rant
woogie fart
soothing sayers
with random sounds
when they bother to listen
under the table of the day
with drums
that play and play
turn centuries into a day
and teach yes and no
in ways surreptitious
and so blatant

woogies come on
with poetry and
end up in trance
eat the salt of the earth
in ways that generate plenitude
and sweet braggadocio smiles
and will the underbelly be soft
with the plight
that pleases sassy
and strong even
in the morning's urgencies

woogies come   in both sexes
and all
have been known to
have a ball at funerals
and sink into the earth
as easily as swim or fly
and try the patience
of contrived equations
and sing the praises

of all the lords
in serendipity
mutations
that grab bank notes
by the corner store
and send them to the coffers
squealing with fright
and tenterhook certainty

woogies are here
and there
and
some place else
name elf and gargantua
within their number
and faint helpless
at a certain smile

they know notes
the repetition of
jams main arteries
with letters of mattering
a broadside
tracing the genealogy
of the cells
to righteous amplitudes
which even feet hear
and now tap
their throes to
in liberating choreographies
on under employment lines

woogies stand above
cant and crave
a little too easily
for their critics

scrambled

that scrambled   scrambling radio
show in my head since the '40's

a theme
i can't quite get to
can't quite get   catch phrase

hero show gesture   and stance
and come on   let's get up   and dance

get outta here jack   the jig's up   kind of image
and magic super man language
and sound effects
and side effects

silent as zombies   written all over your face

the radio   scrambled
show blowing my mind
lone ranger in danger
quick let's get outta here

friday night sneak
out the back door
get into something quick
radio scam action
scrambling

scram   jack armstrong
last seen eating wheaties
in a straight jacket
scrambling for   his strife
on this is your fate

radio imagination

the only station
you ever tune into
that's the wrong one
all the time

and likes you   too

unlimited

herds of incomprehensibilities
stampeding across your brain
and quick as a flash   a telegram

there's more coming
and you can't get outta there
and there can't get outta you

likes you   too much

you're the only one   on the block
who tunes into this question man
so who can you tell the next day
in school   answer boy

soapy opera watched
ears showing like uncle bob's
manic chimpanzee's

your radio is showing   zip it up quick
the authorities can't stand   scrambled

things are falling   a part

i don't just mean the center which
some physicists and other philosophers
of atomic activities   claim
doesn't exist any how

but a bolt drops   here
at my feet   a nut and
there   higher insurance costs
lowering expectations with faulty cranes

these days
when you say this is lacking in quality
you're not even called elitist

things actually are falling apart

one day
it will be buildings instead of people
and other people

because their accountants order them

will decide there is an emergency
to be considered

jones town

so you listen

you keep one ear to the wind
you hide your face from

you are van gogh   slowly

drawing pictures of soft blades
lopping off concrete pigments

one by one by one
close to a thousand times

in the inner ear you hear falling   slowly

you look down   softly
making sure your feet are still there

the other ear
hears tramping protest

whose city THERE

THERE is a drug store
on the south west corner of
16th and valencia at
the bus stop of the #26 and
if you stand THERE for
a long time on a nice day and
look across the intersection   catty cornered
THERE is a space where
a building could be   was   and   will be

it's only a matter of time
THERE will be a building
at least one building THERE
      (there's all ready a parking lot
        down the street and around the corner to the right
        that's how come you know
        it'll be a building
        not a parking lot)

if you stand THERE for
a long time during a nice day and
watch who looks into this space where
THERE could be   was   and   will be a building
you'll see people stare down   lookup   staredown   and look
                                                                              up and

go about THERE business
waiting for a bus or
going to the bank or the post office or
going to get a burrito or
going to get lunch at the sincere cafe
which used to be housed in a building
that used to provide living space for people where
it is now empty

how long ago this space
provided decent living for
people who could afford the
rent is a matter for historians

on jan 18th 1972
the building that was THERE
then was cited by the city of sf dept of public works
for 38 code violations including
hazardous wiring
lack of sprinklers in the basement and
over crowding   toomanypeopleintoolittlespace
to make how much money for
how many other people and for
how long is unclear for
sure the gartland apartments didn't start
out as a fire trap slum and
it wasn't all ways just
real poor people livng THERE
some too old some too crippled to
spend a lot of time driving
around the city of sf looking
for just the right place to
settle

it took the city of sf dept of public works
only 8½ months to issue a report
out lining the violations
which is probably a lot shorter time than
it took for the violations to develop while
the city of sf dept of public works
was doing what?
to let that number of violations pile up
    (all so a matter for historians
        . . . of urban neglect . . .)

and then it took
the city of sf dept of public works
only one month shy of two years
to condemn   not bring about code compliance by the owners
for the benefit of the people
who were paying full amounts of rent

it took the city of sf dept of public works
only one month shy of two years to condemn
the gartland apartments

the city of sf will evict you and me
at tax payers' cost much more quickly

when the owners of
the building that used to be THERE
appealed the ruling
the city of sf abatement appeals board gave
the owners 90 days to comply and
in nov of 1975 set a trial date
to prosecute the owners for
non compliance on jan 26th 1976
all most 4 years to the day of
the first citation

if after you stand THERE for
a long time and watch to see
who looks who notices
some do some don't
some will some won't and you
get real curious your self and
if you're fast enough to beat the change of
the walk to don't sign twice
you can look into down
into the empty space and you
can see underneath bricks   and tires   and wine bottles
and city drift wood

the land
right here in the city
you can actually see the
land

whose land is this
who's to say what's to happen here in
this empty space where
the gartland apartments used to be till
they were destroyed by fire
some still say it was arson

and twelve people died in the night of
instant black lung and searing flesh on
dec 12th 1975   before the case
could come to court

whose land is this
who is to say what is to happen here
why not the people
for the people who
are citizens of this
abstract entity
the city of sf

THERE is here

DEVOLUTION

we used to dance
we used to dance
to the drums
to the drums
to the drum drum drumming

pulsating knowledge
stroke and stomp steps
of flowing science
smoking hows of rhythm
imagining whys of
delicate proportion

we used to dance to learn
we used to dance and learn
to the drumming and the hum,
that wove the selves and the stars
in to bright black eyes' vision

stomp and stroke
pulsating language
all around flow of
rhythm and balance
song of smoking hows ablaze
o' imaginations' rigorous ways

then this
great cosmic joke
us not nimble enough
to evade this snare
of in human yoke

the hot chain of identity
and long drink of serial
symbols washed down with lies
we learned to earn
then yearn for

constructing identities
and new local visions
this transcendant process
of militancy and mind trap
we wove our selves
in and out of

these mysteries of land lords
and history books of such
textual intricacy and
ordered by the dean of the day erudition
we missed the dance
and never noticed
while we learned

to in scribe foot notes
with fragments of bone
integrate identities
that switch hats
with dramatic celerity
and sign checks
with the third hand

we huffed and we puffed and
we gladly be came the house

who is this act of torture the order for

why is the whip in the hand of the priest and the diplomat

the stop sign thief runs amucking
just down the block
and why do the officers all ways
get here late where
one time even
four little girls were . . .
WERE WHAT?
DID
you say
in a church
in birmingham

another fact
too trite
for the time
of the numbed gardenia
and rancid seas

three feet away
some chiseler
liberates life boats
to fill his prescriptions
for grosse pointe tease

miami beach cubanos
offer to enslave when
the price is right
if sugar sucks green backs
behind the curtain
. . . SI !

SI ! . . .
SEE
SEE WHAT IS HAPPENING

DICK
HERE
JANE
NOW
WHAT IS HAPPENING
HERE
SEE SPOT RUN
NOW

what shall we do
with our new definitions
here staring at
the traces of quick lime
on the edges
of the trenches and ditches
on the lawn
of this trustee
and that turn coat
who might approach
at any moment

and the apple cart is tipping over

how do these wheres
fit us
where
do any body sit
in this house
over looking these
planes of dessication
broken pipes of
dream on dappled
desire that
never got there

how do we
move over
in here where
moon beams cower
in groups of ten
at noon
and the guard
feeds us a spoon
of melting ice
that all ways splashes
our tuxedoes

what happened to the dance
. . . jack
what happened
to the dance

how sweet it is

the revolution tried to bludgeon me   with commitment
told me to be free   with each crack on the head

the revolution had no medical plan   for my aching skull
and the man's doctors prescribed 9 to 5 and
lots of greenbacks for my headache

the revolution told my old lady to be free
didn't tell her how to relate to me   nor me to her
except give up some head once in a while   for liberation

the revolution shot me and my friends up with media
hand in hand with the networks' contingency plans and
left me here with a spoonful of words

the revolution calls a squall   a typhoon
                        a shopkeeper   a tycoon
                        a poem   an anthem
turns rhythm into syncopation   and creation into proletarian news
trains cadets to sing the blues   in make believe ballroom time
and   gives the marshalls degrees in critical arts   and science

the revolution missed the people   in its zeal
poured caffeine into the finest crystal
made a killing in blue jeans
dungareed the social register in dingy splendor
charging their public accounts with the masses' ragged debts
and passed judgement in lynch mob terms
from university chairs reserved for the asses of the classes

the revolution turned the myth of the man into everyday truth
taking us out of we
made each difference a deep fault we fell into
with only the weak fibre of me   to pull ourselves up with
gave starry equations in splendid incantation
planting a collective maypole in the ruts of spring
polling universal need with the central committee's questionnaire

the revolution washed the brain out of my head   in the name of our
                                                                                         liberty

the revolution bought bentleys and cocaine
and private sets in the california hills
jamming all night with freedom now and the 6 coquettes
caviar on their nipples   gyrating on peppermint sticks
coming to tell the truth to the city   when tomorrow gets here
if they come to get us in the morning

the revolution sent strollers on a long march   without a map
mixed black and brown into a 3rd concoction anyone can handle
and not have to ask is this the real thing
and liberated space from everybody's closet
said come on out   the mace is fine
from poolside havens sipping black russians
with a publisher or two fawning and feignting   a jab of reverence
at each toast

the revolution stashed panama reds and acapulco golds
backyard greens in a natural crock   and
sent the brave into the jungle and the catacombs
to establish the territoriality of identity in the libraries of the cosmos
while workers jammed pension funds with rich pollution
and ate steaks sprinkled with ethnic jokes

the revolution made a hole in me
trying to make a whole of us
that only we can fill

the revolution is you and me listening to each other
filling holes with our guts and making wholes with our love

the revolution is that steamshovel lyricism
we are running back home to get
now that we've been had and been a hullabaloo
and everything else we thought we were missing

the revolution is our bloody love song
on nobody's hit parade but our own

s & m lover

sweet storm   troopers of love
salient like malignant stars
pinioned on jet turbulence
ivory studs piercing ebony swirls
seizing the inner eye
o' rapine dragon lady pillager
of crook'd finger
night gypsy talents
wielding the slither
put the whip cream on my iris
and eat out the stars

we used to sit like this

we used to set our selves in places
together with such otherness
we did no justice to the special knowledge
we shared when we were there

when we were there

we some times used to sit like this
just like this together in our apartness
sharing apartments of selves with abandon
in spaces that choked with love
and not enough sun light

i know when we were there

though i could bring you no pearls
to string a set of sweet dabbles with
and i had searched well and hard
i could say hello a little better
to strangers pets and pests too

you searched in the stars
with such loving eyes
i wept alone

we could sit there some times

in just this kind of embrace
of time and selves and place
and no glue   not a piece of tape
the stores all closed for the week end
and we only had four arms
amongst our countless hearts

in this place where we used to sit

all by our selves and each awkward
with a loneness and that kind of love
gyrating on lines of hope and struggle
and so be it

so be it there

we set our selves up
mirrors of glance with gymnastic graces
and touched and tumbled and ran and touched
and touched

ran to touch the run away selves who
all ways knew how to search for truth
and other things to touch and run to
and from

i sit in this place

some times reflecting
balanced precariously on the edge of memory
and reflected

CAPRICORN

in the basement of our old house in brooklyn
in the basement past the coal dust
in the basement past the old furnace
our father had converted to oil after or was it
during the second world war
past the furnace that one day
exploded
leaving a hole the size of a cannon ball
in the asbestos and piss poor plaster job
filling the whole house with smoke and
harsh sweet burnt oil fumes

the furnace the fire department decided wasn't
a fire hazard in spite of the hole in it

in the basement past the pile of
stakes and puptents
canvass and canteens
bandoleers and gas masks
mustard gas covering and helmets
knapsacks messkits insignia
theater of war ribbons
musty khaki mess mostly

past the pile of junk
where we used to create
each and every battle of
the second world war
right off the radio
hot out of the n y times

the pile of junk that our uncle
sent to us from hawaii
where he had gone
after the fbi explained to him the advantages
of officers candidate school over leavenworth

waheenies and administration beat forced labor any day he
                                                    thought
he sent us pictures of flower bedecked sweethearts to prove it
him smiling like clark gable
gold bars gleaming
holstered .45 popping in our heads

past the pile of mush and pulp
my first collection of baseball record books
our mother had hid there
to keep my head in the right textbooks
that pile of mush made by a broken drain pipe
that flooded the whole cellar and put out the furnace

past that pile
stood an old wooden door planked like a cargo hatch
opening to a wine cellar
built when the neighborhood was white and respectable
the old wooden door creaked like inner sanctum mystery
room empty but for dust and dirt
and old steamer trunk
symptom of lying splendor
rusting in place

in the basement past this pile
past that pile of interesting irrelevance
in the wine cellar unlike our grandma's filled
with shiney new garbage cans of sugar and
shelves of canned delicacies
hoarded to beat the rationing
it was empty but for dust
the trunk and the echoing creaky door

past ths emptiness
through the well constructed
stone by stone mortared wall
past the dust and dirt was
a beach i knew well

white sand triumphed by red sand bluffs
pink wild roses
blackberries blueberries and wild raspberries
we used to pick for grandma to make pies with

white sand leading you to a rushing into the bay creek
our parents and friends used to crab and eel in
before they settled down to their mysterious all
night nude drunken brash beach parties
we could never attend until
we were old enough

white sand getting wetter and wetter
softer and softer until you
could hear yourself crunching
and crackling fiddler crab holes
looking at your great size
even at eleven years old

emerald beach flies buzzed and bit
you slapping them away continuously
and it was no great trouble   fun in fact
you looking towards an interminable stretch of
tidelands marsh green that stretched you knew
all the way to the easthampton golf club
where stuart tripped into the mud one sweaty afternoon
collecting cattails to dry and burn
to keep away the mosquitoes or so we told ourselves
any excuse for an adventure

crossing the rushing into the bay creek
played into more white sand

only here in the basement
only here in the wine cellar
only here past the well constructed
stone by stone mortared wall
where there used to be a vast
to the eye and ear tidelands marsh
was an endless desert
that led me on and on

strangely trudging inexhaustable
both of us   me and the desert
the sun always bright scorching
daring my searching eyes
only horizon to see

white sand level as the base of a triangle
stretching in lazy intent
and it really didn't matter
i walked it   lord how i walked it
inexhaustable searching eyes
sun in searing yellow orange red white
always in the same spot

i walked it   lord i walked it
alone trudging gazing searching
listening to the silence of my feet on the sand
blistering bearable footage of quiet intent
and it really didn't matter that i
didn't know where i was or where i was going
because i was there and i was doing it
no questions asked

the sun looked at me and i looked at it
there was no room for agreement or disagreement
i was doing it no questions asked

the sand white hot sun sodden and silent
was doing it no questions asked

and that's what it was
no mirages   no temptations
just doing it drily   endlessly
for a long time in a day that lasted a lifetime
a millenium an epoch

doing it on the desert
in the sun that always burst
from the same spot in the sky
about the size of an onrushing
just about to collide planet

on the white sands
that told you nothing forever

until it occurred to me

it was uncanny

i didnt have to repeat it   in my head
nothing changed except my direction

i had not chosen it
nor had i not chosen it
it was not chosen

it was a change of direction
on this eerie desert
i watched myself come back from

the same way i had gone
no questions asked
the sun in the eyes of me looking at me
coming back to where i didn't know

i was looking at me doing it
only horizon to see
sun always bright scorching
daring my searching eyes

no mirage   no temptation
endless stretching white silent sands
level gritty perfect plane
inexhaustable   both of us

no room for emptiness or fullness
i was doing it endlessly
leading me on an on
looking at myself
strangely trudging

. . . and the creek whispered
and the creek whispered
and the creek whispered
i was doing it   crossing it
inexhaustable and quietly
glad i was doing it

swift bayward tug
at my knees calves ankles toes
and white sand of a beach i knew well

past the creaky door echoing
the statistical mush
the slumped puptent
the furnace with a hole in the side

past war games and coal dust
up creaky wooden always theratening to betray you
cellar stairs into the bright baby blue hallway
leading to the wrought iron gate i walked through

into the streets of brooklyn
to play another game of you
show me yours and i'll show you mine

inexhaustable

être rejeté
dans les vents fous
encore
moi   moi-même
sans le premier "d'accord"

dieu
ce monstre-ci

et un ange
aussitôt qu'un baiser
commence à jouer
siroco

et je suis homme éternel

nous sommes
nous sommes